BANKS:

THE CAUSE AND CURE OF RECESSION

BANKS:
THE CAUSE AND CURE OF RECESSION

THRES. JOSEPH KAROTTUKUNNEL

Copyright © 2012 by Thres. Joseph Karottukunnel.

ISBN:	Softcover	978-1-4691-9103-4
	Ebook	978-1-4691-9104-1

All rights reserved. No part of this book may be reproduced or transmitted in any form or by any means, electronic or mechanical, including photocopying, recording, or by any information storage and retrieval system, without permission in writing from the copyright owner.

This book was printed in the United States of America.

To order additional copies of this book, contact:
Xlibris Corporation
1-888-795-4274
www.Xlibris.com
Orders@Xlibris.com

CONTENTS

Introduction 7

Chapter I 9

Chapter II: The Role of Banks in the Economy 23

Chapter III: A Recession Free Economy 29

Chapter IV: Banks and the Economy 35

INTRODUCTION

This book is all about recession, the economy, and the impact of the banking system on the economy. Recession is a term people in general would not want to hear about. It is a term makes people think negatively about the economic system. The solution to recession usually nobody knows but all are anxious about the consequences of recession, how it is going to affect their day to day living, and what do with the bleak future right in front of them. They all know that a Recession is not a joke; it is accompanied by lay-offs, unemployment, business-shut downs, bankruptcy, foreclosures, low-standard of living, and the consequent social evils like divorces, suicides, break-ins, bank robbery, homelessness, and other sad things. So it is a scary term and in effect even before the actual recession begins people become mentally depressed both the consumers and producers and sometimes the government sector too. Though the economic advisors of the government knows that recession is not yet hit the Economy, because of the over-anxiety of the people, the government officials sometimes have to admit in front of people that the Recession is at hand. This is an anxiety generated recession. But somehow or other eventually producers, consumers and the governing system get caught into that and most of the time they forget to look into the cause of Recession and from where it started and what steps to be taken to block it at the earliest and the easiest way.

CHAPTER I

An economy rooted and grounded in a strong and stable banking system will never ever undergo a long Recession because Recession originates from the banking system and then it contaminates the whole economic system.

Now the simple question comes in everybody's mind is how can that be taken place? This is how it goes.

Banks get connected with all the individuals and families through the promotion of savings and loans. Individuals find Bank as a safe haven for their financial stability. They get connected with the bank based on their financial need. For instance, a young couple from Chicago, Linda and John, moved to Atlanta, Georgia with a dream to bring up their two kids away from the hustle and bustle of the city and to educate them in a suburban neighborhood. Linda works as a Registered Nurse and John is a licensed X-Ray Technician. They both worked hard for ten years in Chicago and had a bank balance of two hundred thousand dollars in their savings account when they moved to Atlanta.

As soon as they moved to Atlanta they went to the bank closer to their apartment to open a checking account in that bank so that they can get direct deposit to their account from their jobs. Both of them got a job in the Hospital' in Atlanta. Mean time they had an intense desire to buy a decent house in a quiet neighborhood. The houses in Atlanta fascinated them. As they both got full-time jobs in the hospital, they decided to buy a house in Atlanta. They went to the Bank again to discuss the matter with the loan officer and they elaborated the matter in such a way that the loan officer in the bank could find out their present and future plans. John had a plan to buy a gas station and a convenient store if everything works out well with the Housing loan. When John was working as an X-ray Technician, he had this dream to become a business man and then to become a millionaire. The Bank could sense this really well from them.

The Bank officer was thrilled with this idea and gave them all kinds of possibilities to take a loan for both the House and the Business which John was dreaming about. Linda and John had already two hundred thousand dollars savings in their Chicago Bank. The Atlanta Bank officer encouraged them to open a savings account in the Bank to move that amount to Atlanta. They thought it was a good idea and they opened a savings account and then the bank officer also tempted John by saying that when John's business is about to start they will help John to start a business account too. John and Linda left the Bank with a heart full of happiness thinking as if all their dreams are full-filled.

The financial accomplishment story begins here. The next day after they met the loan officer in the Bank they called the realtor in that area to look for a house. And they could locate a house with one hundred thousand dollars down.

The Bank was really happy. The real deal and closing was done within a month.

The couple got their dream house in the suburbs of Atlanta and their children started to go to a private school where tuition is fairly high. So they got a good school and a good house, but one more dream was left for John and that is a good business-a gas station and a convenient store.

Two weeks after they moved to the house, one afternoon, and the loan officer at the Bank called John at home saying that a guy who has an account with the Bank has a convenient store and a gas station for sale and John thought it was God sent. He rushed to the bank to meet that guy who is selling the business. The loan officer of the bank turned out to be a facilitator to the conversation between the owner of the gas station and the would-be buyer is John. In fact, the loan officer accompanied them to the business when John wanted to see the business.

Finally, in two days time John decided to place a contract to buy the business for half a million dollars on condition to get an approval from the bank. In a month time both parties agreed at the terms and conditions the loan was approved with buyer seemed superb because in one of the conversations on the phone the bank officer told John that the business was actually worth a million dollars.

John thought after moving to Atlanta all his dreams are full filled—he got a half a million dollar house which he thought is a mansion, his two children got a private school which he thinks the school is the best choice for his children and beyond all that he got a million dollar worth of business just for half a million. In three months time, everything in his dreams became true. John is the owner of a business: He is the owner of a business, he has the house of his dreams and his wife Linda got a full-time job in the Hospital that makes around five thousand dollars every month. Above all John thinks in Atlanta he got the luck to meet the loan officer in the bank who according to John is the best friend he ever met in his whole life.

As days go by, the friendship between John and the loan officer in the bank is strengthened and John was a happy man in every way. One day the loan officer made a friendly visit to the Business of John and passed a message that there is two acres of property lying right across John's business and it was going to be sold. He also mentioned casually that if another gas station comes right opposite to John's business, it could be a threat. To avoid that John could buy that property, he and his business would be saved, guaranteed. John told him that just after a year of buying this property he would not be in a position to buy that property which is worth a million dollars. The loan officer asked him politely to think about it and he left. The matter actually bothered John. Another business coming as a threat to his business actually stayed in his mind as a distraction.

After one week, the loan officer while he was talking to him on the phone asked John whether he can stop by at the bank and also mentioned that he may have a new idea about that property. As his best friend requested him to go there John did not think much and went to the bank. Two best friends meeting and discussing future business plans was a thrill for John. This time the loan officer gave him another idea to make money and get rich. He told him about a fantastic idea which would help him to be a millionaire in a month time. That is to take a second mortgage on his home and business and buy the million dollar property and eventually develop that property for himself and make it a multimillion dollar business. What a perfect idea" John went back with a heart filled with hope and happiness and deep in his heart he felt that he had achieved all that because second mortgage is not a problem at all. His wife was little reluctant at first but later she also thought that the loan officer is a good friend and once it comes from him it is okay.

Now, one year after moving to Atlanta, they are on the Road to become a millionaire. With all happiness, they decided to take a second mortgage on their home and business and finally buy the million dollar land situated right opposite to John's store.

They started making payments for both the loans on the house and business plus the loan on the new property, payments on the car, tuition for both their children with food and utility bills added to it. For three months they could somehow manage that. But business began to become slow, Linda started working overtime children's tuition bills delayed and stress mounted up. At that point credit cards helped them to survive. As a consequence1 credit card companies started making friendly phone calls, to remind Linda and John about their duty to pay the bills. With struggle they somehow managed to pay the bills.

But in that struggle John got a heart attack. Because of his wife's job medical insurance covered all his hospital bills and with sheer luck he survived the attack. The family as a whole began to move into a troubled environment. Income from the store began to decline because of John's absence from the store. Linda continued her overtime to cover the expenses. The jovial spirit in the family is crushed down. Bills from the pharmacy now are added up to the other mortgage bills. John's best friend in the bank has been moved to another branch. Now John's family actually faced a deep recession emotionally, financially, and in health condition. In a year time, he got everything foreclosed-the store, the million dollar property and the house. They decided to pull out the children from the private school and put them in a public school. They got a low rent house to make it affordable for them at present.

Now the whole family is poor financially poor in health and poor in spirit. In Chicago they could accumulate two hundred thousand dollars in savings with no debts and for that they did ten years of hard work. After coming to Atlanta they did everything right in the beginning. The house . . . the store . . . and the school for the kids they picked real well. Their dream to become a millionaire was on the road to go. The foundation laid was really perfect. Two years after reaching Atlanta, they lost practically everything and more than that they went into deep debts. Yet Linda's job is there, and John also can go to work. The economic growth in this particular family is collapsed in a year time and now they are trying to build up something from scratch.

What is the cause of this recession in the family of John and Linda? It is the bank. This recession is originated from the bank. The bank noticed that there is a two hundred thousand savings in the account of this couple and in the obsession for profit, the bank wanted to use this couple by taking advantage of their dreams. There is a winning incentive, "in the banks to make profit by ignoring the basic principles of economic growth which is justice and fairness."

Once the economy is prosperous and people in general seem to be well off banks get wild ideas which are "greed" in frozen form.

Usually there is a saying that at the end of prosperity there is a recession and that is a natural consequence. The Economists, politicians, and the general public; all of them agree on this statement. This is an age-old saying backed by several business cycles in the history. It is stated that business can go only in a cycle. In other words, all business owners have to face a recession in their business and they better get ready for that.

Business cycle and recession a situation where even babies and older people have to pay a price for it. The question is who perpetrates this recession?
What is the driving force behind this? The people in every nation easily come to a conclusion that the leadership in a nation failed. If it is the American people they~ within no time, turn to the President of the Nation and point their fingers at him saying that it is the President of this country who caused this Recession.
Immediately, the Congress and the Senate start discussions and make all derogative remarks about the party who has the majority and the sitting President. The conclusion is this way. The inefficiency and failure of the Administration is the cause of the Economic insecurity in the nation. The chairman of the Federal Reserve System has to take lot of heat because of the financial failure. Now the big question remains as who started this big mess?

The answer is going to be very very strange. This whole thing is started from a "greedy bank." During the time of prosperity "greed" comes in as a visitor to the Economy. It comes and goes around as a well-wisher to make everything little more prosperous and stable. It is like the bank officer who came to visit John's Business and helped him to take a second mortgage on the business and on the house to grab a million dollar property with no cash flow and putting John in a fantasy world where he will collect millions by developing that property. Look what happened? In that deal John was pulled into recession and eventually destruction. Instead, John would have been very well off if he had only one mortgage with the Bank and there would have been a stable and healthy growth for his life and financial situation. Surprisingly, in two years time he collapsed to ground zero-his health, assets, savings, everything came to the dust.

A complete chaos crept into his life situation and then he decided to start all over again to save his family and the future of his children. Here we see a business cycle operating in John's life. Who caused it? The Bank. In the beginning bank helped him to grow and then with the inappropriate advice to the client Bank helped him to collapse to the dust. Why? Because greed took over the decisions of the bank and they passed it to the business sector. Yet the

Business sector trusts the bank as the protector and defender of their assets. So they follow immediately what this bank tells them to do. Although it is a second . . . third or fourth mortgage . . . the business is ready to follow the bank's advice because they do not know that the bank is making them a slave as the "Merchant of Venice" in Shakespeare's book.

Now the well off business man John emerged to a state of foreclosed Business, foreclosed house, foreclosed million dollar property, a huge debt, laid off workers, delayed credit card bills, slow credit and a failed health. Yet with the optimism left in his inherent personality, he has decided to work hard, rebuild his life, family and dream again. This is what everybody calls "Recovery."

This state of affairs most Economists call it a "Business cycle" but would be better to call it a "Business circle" created artificially by the "Lousy Advice" from the local Banks. The "greed factor" operated from one bank made the life of a bunch of hard working people in a "circle" where they work hard again with a dream and finally they will be going in a circle reaching nowhere but never stop working to take care of a stack of bills.

The greed does not stop with one bank; it goes to all the banks including the "Federal Reserve System" and through the Fed it takes a flight to visit all the central Banks in the world like the "Witch" in the Snow White story. Now the national Economy and the whole world go in a "circle." And the economic advisers in every country would call it "global Recession."

CHAPTER II

The Role of Banks in the Economy

Banks constitute the epic center of an economic system. It is the brain that guides, manages and maintains an economy. A strong Banking system with no malice is the foundation on which the whole super structure of the economy is built. The local banks if they work based on the economic law which insists "Justice and fairness" in every step of the economic activity which involves production consumption, distribution plus international trade, or transactions in the international economy. The calamity caused by recession as a consequence of "greed" could be completely eliminated from the domestic and global economy.

An economy deep rooted in the "Law of Economics" will never show symptoms of Recession. The excess and intense desire for profit in the banking system pulls the banks to the old usury era and the "survival of the fittest" slogan of the 19th century which brought the "Great Depression" of the 1930's. The world population paid a big price for the disastrous and treacherous Economic Era. Adam smith's theory was based on the "Law of Economics" but it could not suggest something for a technologically wired economy or a fast growing society.

Robert Malthus also could envision a society which is dominated by farmers plough and bullocks. As a result he thought population growth was going to be a burden to the coming generation. As a consolation Malthus presumed that nature itself will find out a means to get rid of the excess population from the planet and that is through natural calamities like earthquakes, famines, war and off such other occurrences. Definitely Malthus was not aware of tsunami. The chronic pessimistic mind of Malthus even predicted a "doom day" for the food supply in the world. Being overwhelmed by population growth and with his old "arithmetic and geometric growth" principle Malthus could not envisage the unimaginable technological growth in the future and the consequent employment opportunities in the global economy. So Malthus developed and published a pessimistic message about population growth and the consequent recession in the world.

But Keynesian theory brought hope to a distressed world economic system John Maynard Kaynes explained that the supply side economics and the demand side economics when it comes to an imbalance how the fiscal and monetary system can set the system in a balance. Deficit financing came up to the economic scene as a rescue measure to fill the under production at the GDP level and to correct the imbalance in supply and demand. The fiscal and monetary policies of the government in cooperation with the central bank worked real well to tackle the depression of the 1930's Keynesian theory worked for the twentieth century economy. But today in the 21st century does it going to work? Those days it worked for a closed economic system the whole scenario changed today. 21st century faces an open economy which is global.

The role that the bank has to play in an economic system is all the more emphasized in this global economy. No matter how hard the fiscal system works to level the economic imbalance, the master key is with the banking system, and hence the diagnosis, prognosis and solution should ultimately come from the Banking system.

But, many times the imbalance is originated from the bank and through the multiplier effect if ravages the whole economic system. It contaminates and pollutes the Economic activities all over; previously it was affected by the domestic economy, now it goes beyond the Domestic economy and can go globally. It is kind of an Enron syndrome. The Bug doesn't stop with one company, one bank or with one nation; it can go beyond imagination because of the fastest technology today.

In the fate 1930's the Fiscal policy worked miracles and salvaged the world economy. The system is not receptive or effective in the modern economic world because every economic activity today affects the global economy. The international trade, for instance, today is not in the control of the government in the total form because of the technological growth. As a result, business regulations by the government could be delayed and it cannot catch up with volume of trade.

But every transaction has something to do with the bank. Now the question is whether to follow the Keynesian fiscal policy criterion to measure GDP and/or GNP or to take another route to detect the problem of balancing the budget. A stable economic policy is the primary requirement for a stable economic system.

In a global economy government's policies are to be more lenient and organized in such a way that it should enable the banking system works efficiently and let the government has a clear watch over the banking system to make sure that greed never takes over the banking system.

CHAPTER III

A Recession Free Economy

Is it possible to have a recession-free economy? Yes. It is not a myth and the answer does not come from a Utopian realm of the mind. If Banks by all means stay away from the satanic force of "greed," the word Recession would go to the archives of the Economic system in the coming century. Does that mean bank has to be turned out to be a charitable institution? No. It is not true. Not only that banking industry would be thriving in a clean environment where banks work earnestly for the welfare of the people; the economic growth and well-being of the individual citizens, families and the nation all over. The regular cash flow in the bank increases in large volumes and the normal profit based on "justice and fairness" make them financial giants.

Accumulation of wealth based on the law of Economics creates trust in the banking system, in the financial system, in the Economic system and it sets a path in the overall system a path of confidence in the social, cultural and political system. A strong and uncorrupt banking system is the brain and the nerve center of the Economy. It is like a well-built highway in the Road system where you get all the exits to the different aspects of growth in the economy. A corruption free banking system and structure is like a big umbrella where every economic unit can grow in a healthy and stable way.

How to do that? Bank regulations are to be re-organized in such a way that even a small child knows what the requirements for getting a mortgage loan from the Banks. To get a mortgage loan from the bank a twenty percent down for the good credit and a forty percent down for the bad credit would give the people an idea that to own a home they have to come up with some money upfront and then what rate the interest carries for good and bad credit holders. They thus get an idea about how much money they have to accumulate to get a house in their dreams. Then the house will reflect the eligibility and hard work of a person which adds certainty to the housing market and the financial system.

Though uncertainty is designated as part of the Economic system; to create trust in the financial system we have to add as much certainty as we can to the economic system to make the people active participants in the economy.

Anything that the banking system does should vitalize the incentive of the people to work hard with stress and uncertainty the least. Please don't let the people work in an uncertain system although uncertainty is part of the human existence.

The success of an economic system depends on how much certainty can be created in an uncertain world. That trust is created by the banks. This job of trust creation in cooperation with the government is the job entrusted to a strong banking system. More than ever banks are extremely important in the present and coming centuries. It is a noble function bank has to perform in the economy.

It is a function goes beyond profit accumulation. To perpetuate economic stability the bank has to stand in the front line of every valid financial transaction. And through the multiplier effect it vibrates the whole economy. Bank, in other words, is the originator, patron and perpetrator of economic stability. If "greed"' dominates the banking system business cycle and then business "circle" would be the end result. And people suffer which politicians and the people at large would call it the period of Recession and depression. This corruption in the banking system determines the length of recession. On the other hand if the banking system almost every day monitors the Economy with an intention to make it grow they can correct the deviations and make the system grow undisturbed.

A reckless banking system with its deep desire to use the economy to make profit depicts the typical Enron syndrome and works to dissemble the entire superstructure of the banking industry. Ipso facto it undermines the process of evaluating real GDP. The outcome is going to be in two ways: either GDP is overvalued and that is inflation or undervalued which is deflation. The entire economy could be in a state of inflation by creating an unusual difference in real GDP and nominal GDP. If a loan is not backed up by real security system then banks inject inflation directly to the economic system. Unsecured loans of any kind are dangerous to the economy. At times it can end up in hyper inflation.

Unbridled lending activity of banks obsessed with profit can generate inflation that disrupts the financial security of the individuals and eventually the society as a whole. Like a deadly hurricane it can cause damages in the business sector and other economic units on its way to go forward.

Once the economy is ravaged by inflation, the blame goes to the fiscal policy of the government because of the deficit financing. But government borrowing is not much to be blamed because it is based on a valuable security which is the government bonds. A productive loan helps to accumulate wealth on both sides, that is the borrower and the lender will accumulate wealth. The discrepancy between the nominal value and the real value if it is too wide.! then both sides are going to lose and inflation is the outcome of that loan. The zero down mortgage lending with a very high interest rate only helped to sow the seeds of inflation in the economy. Both the lender; the bank, and the borrower; the owner of the house, were not accumulating any value to their side OF course, the bank was getting bigger amounts of money as mortgage payments but the real value was going down. The borrower was getting nothing because the real value of the house was much lower than the nominal value or the face value of the house.

Did the Housing Market collapse in the United States? The answer is no. But something attached to the Housing Market did collapse. It is nothing but the plastic super structure built by the banks on top of the bricks, that fell off. The inflated super structure created by the bank fell off. And the Housing Market scared everybody because many of them did not realize the difference between the plastic-superstructure and the real Housing Market. The Economy is still not out of that shock. The real Economy is in good health but dormant because of the shock.

CHAPTER IV

Banks and the Economy

An economy if it wants to do away with the frequent occurrence of the business cycle or a prolonged state of Recession it should be on a strong leadership rooted in a sound financial system originated and perpetuated by a "greed-free" financial planning and not by a "user-oriented" financial goal. It is the bank's mission and responsibility to see that the individuals and families in an economy is growing and the growth momentum is adequately supported by an equity-based financial foundation—to be more specific, a financial base with equal opportunity and equity is the sole means to build up a strong banking system.

Once the banks are inefficient, feeble-structured with no ability to reach out to people to understand the financial strengths and weaknesses of the people in the area where the bank is located, then that bank is going to be a colossal failure in a short period of time.

The first and foremost thing a bank should do is to teach the public how the Law of Economics works and what it means to each family and each business.

Once the people know this important law they know how to accumulate wealth in the most healthy way where cheating and greed is not an essential component of economic well-being and economic growth. In the absence of cheating economic growth is smooth and retardation of growth is impossible.

Banks have a special responsibility to each family who is trying to get a home and to each person who is trying to build up a business of his own. As the first step banks have to teach them the consequences of too much debts. Then show them how they can build up wealth by reducing debts. The payments the bank can be delayed or may be sometimes stopped if the home owners and business owners are plunged more and more in debts. By charging more and higher late fees and penalties a healthy solution for delayed payments cannot be reached. Instead, the bank should educate people to stay away from late payments at the very first moment they come to the bank for a loan. If the bank thinks late fees are the best means to gain some profit from the customers, eventually the bank may end up getting no money and the only wealth they have is going to be the foreclosed homes, foreclosed businesses and a debt-stricken population hanging around them looking for a chance to rob the bank to make a living.

So to build a morally upright society, banks have a special role to play. The gradual addition to credit card and other debts including the late payments in the bank can take away the incentive for balancing the persona' finance and bad debts and personal indifference to accounting can creep up which is diametrically damaging to individual economic growth and the general Economy as a whole.

Keynesian concept of deficit financing is good for the running of the government but it is bad for personal financing. In order to achieve personal economic growth balancing the budget is a must and often a surplus budget should be the rule of law in the family and not deficit budget. A deficit budget in the family only helps them to go in a circle and after some time the whole family will be trapped in that circle and finally become bankrupt. Thus when there is business cycle in the economy as a whole, the families in general, are going in a "business circle." Families can avoid this to some extent by setting up a plan for themselves. They have to set their life style first calculate the amount of money required for that style of living and then find out the means to reach that goal.

Never ever try to set a life style based on the credit cards or second or third mortgage on their homes. A second part time job would rather help the family to keep a stable budget than a loan on their home. A debt carries stress anyway.

There is a direct relationship between stress, debts and happiness in the family, other things remaining equal. The more the debts, the more the stress and lesser the happiness. The mental stress caused by debts can even separate the family members. It can even take them to a level of economic breakdowns. Here the local banks can serve as a great strength to keep the family closer by educating them how to stay away from added debts and how to build a healthy financial system in the family by reducing debts and increasing their cash flow. In other words, the local banks can take it as a service to the community by helping families in that local area to build up assets with less debts. The bank is the one ultimately benefitted by that. As the families get rich the banks get richer. The stronger financially the families are the more the strength of the banks financially.

Many people and families know how to make money but only very few know how to manage the finance. The crucial job here for the banks is to educate the families and teach them how to manage their funds.

It is the bank's responsibility to see that the families and businesses in their region are well placed by strong financial foundation. A strong and healthy financial neighborhood based on "justice and fairness" will strengthen the bank financially and socially. Once the bank is ready to serve the community with an intention to build up a healthy financial society, the bank becomes the most trusted authority and source of Economic growth and stability. If the bank wants to step on the community and use them for the profit, then the bank is injecting recession to individual families and businesses and the ultimate outcome would be the presence of a banking institution completely alienated from the financial needs of the community and ends up as a dysfunctional building sitting as a bank in the area.

A financially strong community based on the "Law of Economics" is the back bone of a strong and healthy banking system. In this healthy relationship between banks and the community recession cannot sneak-in, no matter how hard it tries to enter in the system.

A self-analysis by the banks and see what they are doing now and what they should do then a recession-free economy is going to be a reality. There is a common belief supported by the Economists that "Recession" is a "must" and it is a natural consequence after every six years of economic growth.

But a well-built, well balanced and well managed Economic growth will never come to a point of recession. This economy is like an airplane—that is already airborne; it can only go forward unless a very serious engine problem is defected and an emergency landing is required—But even then that problem could be corrected soon and the Aircraft will be Airborne without much delay.

The pilot and mechanic behind this Economic system is a very strong and well developed and disciplined banking system. GDP growth is a natural phenomenon and as the production takes a diversified turn depending on the needs of the people through careful planning every individual finds a place in the system and everybody seem to be making a contribution to the economy. This will happen only in a greed-free setting. If banking system is patronized by a goal oriented and efficient government sector then a Recession cannot creep in and sit there for a long time. It is virtually impossible to cause a disturbance in a strong network between banks and the community.

Today's economy is basically a credit card dominated economy. It is a threat to economic growth. The prosperity overshadowed from 1991-2001 was not a real GDP growth. The investment in stocks was even done on credit cards.

GDP was hijacked by credit card investments. In fact an enron syndrome prevailed all over the Economy making everybody believe that it was prosperity. It was not!! People were just enamored by the millionaire Euphoria. In 2002 what happened was the Law of Economics sets in and shows everybody the actual picture of the economy and people thought it was Recession. It was a wakeup call to the Economic system.

People go around with a wallet full of credit card and buy everything they want with a complacent feeling in their mind and heart that they are millionaires and they have everything they want. The lifestyle and the standard of living was enormously high. But in a short time all these collapsed. Who is responsible for this kind of plastic empire?

It is the banks. People thought it was the recession when real supervision by the banks on the Economic system fails, every aspect of the Economic system comes to a standstill. The big news comes out on television and newspapers about an Economy on the verge of Recession. As soon as it comes out people and the business units become paranoid.

After reading that newspaper Head Line in the morning every business owner goes to his business office with a plan to downsize the business unit in every way possible. The consumers after reading that news in the newspaper makes a decision to cut short their purchase of products as little as possible. The big smoke of pessimism covers the whole Economy. The collapse of the stock market, business lay-offs, some business shut downs here and there ravages the Economy.

Actually the plastic kingdom was in Recession not the real Economy. The real GDP and the Real Economy is still growing. What actually collapsed is the "Bubble" super imposed on the economy by the credit card business is collapsed.

Nothing damaging happened to the Economy. And the Recession was an artificial creation by a set of paranoid business units and consumers.

The Banking system, if it takes the full charge of the macro Economic growth by strengthening the micro Economic units in the Economy then "Recession" will ever disappear from the system and remain as a thing in the past. The unique role the Bank has to play in the Economy is highly demanding but it is the Master Key to the stable, uninterrupted Economic system. The tenacity and vigilance of the Banking system based on the Law of Economics can wipe out Recession from the Economic system for ever.

To achieve this end, the government and the political leadership has to promote, support, and maintain the Banking System healthy, and strong and growing throughout the economy. Banks are the only Economic unit that can have direct access to the Personnel as we" as the family finances, and in that capacity Banks can evaluate fairly well the economic strengths and weaknesses of the economy real well. This knowledge is helpful for the government to make policy decisions in their own capacity and come to useful and effective results that works for the general welfare of the Economy. Thus the government instead of being a threat to the banking system try to be an entrepreneur to protect the welfare of the banking industry and the welfare of the economy as well. Too much control on the banking system can take away the public trust in the Banks and can ruin the financial entity. And the net result is not encouraging for the economy. Shady Banks and usury will pop up and that can in a hidden way root out the strength of the financial system. Then again people start calling it a Recession and it is not a recession but the symptom looks the same. It is a sick economy that cannot catch up with the regular economic transactions.

But once the government and the banks work hand in hand, a healthy and flourishing economy would stay for an unusual length of time.

www.ingramcontent.com/pod-product-compliance
Lightning Source LLC
Chambersburg PA
CBHW021048180526
45163CB00005B/2342